Poetry, Proclamations, and Promises

Series "IT"

Second Edition

Poetry, Proclamations, and Promises

Series "IT"

PMarie

TATE PUBLISHING
AND ENTERPRISES, LLC

Published by Tate Publishing & Enterprises, LLC
127 E. Trade Center Terrace | Mustang, Oklahoma 73064 USA
1.888.361.9473 | www.tatepublishing.com

Tate Publishing is committed to excellence in the publishing industry. The company reflects the philosophy established by the founders, based on Psalm 68:11,
"The Lord gave the word and great was the company of those who published it."

Published in the United States of America

ISBN: 978-1-63063-581-7
1. Inspirational & Religion
2. Poetry/Women Authors
13.11.28

With Special Dedication to True Spiritual Mothers and Fathers for laying solid foundations that led me to grasping, "IT"!

Love Healed

It took strength
It took courage
It took faith
It took prayer
It took the Word
It took meditation
It took correction
It took every verse
It took every chapter
It took every song
It took every hymn
It took every tear
It took the believers
It took the intercessors
It took calling on the name of
  the Lord
It took the anointing
It took the alter
It took those who were called
  by his name
It took those who knew how to
  touch heaven
It took studying
It took reading

It took fasting
It took dancing
It took shouting
It took seeking
It took searching
It took unconditional love
It took the shoulders of others
It took nurturance
It took patience
It took warmth
It took endurance
It took baby steps
It took learning
It took stumbling
It took my mind being renewed
It took being filled with the
 Holy Spirit
It took grace
It took mercy
It took long suffering
It took forgiveness
It took fire
It took power
It took family to love me
   into Healing

Dealing with It

It happened
It's true
It was wrong
I experienced it
I was sadden by it
I didn't understand it
It didn't make any sense
I was snared by it
I was engulfed in it
I was trapped by it
I was lost in it
It was deceiving
I was hurt by it
It was lonely
I wasn't guilty of it
I was frustrated by it
I was sick of it
I didn't know how to stop it
I was ashamed of it
I was confused by it
I was degraded by it
I was uncovered by it
I was exposed by it
I was humiliated by it

I was afraid of it
I was bound by it
I was tricked by it
I was held hostage by it
I was a prisoner of it
It took my voice
I was speechless because of
  it
I felt singled out because
  of it
I felt different because of
  it
I wanted out of it
I was exploited by it
It had me hopeless
I was oppressed by it
It caused me pain
It caused me despair
I lost joy in it
I lost peace in it
It made me crazy
It made me angry
It cost me family
It cost me friends
It made me desperate
It made me shaky

I had low self-esteem
  because of it
It made me unstable
It made me double minded
It made me an emotional
  train wreck
It caused my mood swings
Because of it I had highs
  and lows
It made me hurt the ones
  I loved most
I felt that it would cause
  me to lose my mind
I felt like a failure
  because of it
I felt unworthy because of
  it
I felt unclean because of it
It made me nervous
I didn't feel good enough
  because of it
I felt unworthy because of
  it
I felt unlovable because of
  it

COPING WITH IT

When you've pinned it
When you've tucked it
When you've tried to carry
  it
When you've tried to get
  from beneath it
When you've tried to hide it
When you've tried to cut it
  off
When you've altered it
When you've patched it up
When you walked in the midst
  of it…despite it
When you've danced around it
When you've covered it up
When it sticks out
When it still shows
When you've scrubbed it
When you've washed it and
  it's still not clean
When you've cleaned it and
  it still looks nasty
When you married it
When you slept with it

12

When you lowered your
  standards for it
When you negotiated with it
When you compromised for it
When you sold your soul to
  it
When you settled for it
When you thought you had to
  have it
When you lived with it
When you don't like it
When it causes your heart to
  bleed and your soul to
  leak
When it causes you shame
When it causes you heartache
When it causes you grief
When it stinks
When it's mean
When it's violent
When it has a temper
When it causes you to hate
  yourself
When it causes turmoil
When it won't wait

HOW DO YOU DEAL WITH IT?

When it is jealous
When it is hateful
When it is stubborn
When it is resentful
When it's sneaky
When it doesn't want to see
  you blessed
When it has no remorse
When it is abusive
When it wants to destroy you
When it wants to defeat you
When it steals from you
When it's family
When it's unfaithful
When it wants to babysit
  your children
When it always wants
  something for nothing
When it is unrealistic and
  self -absorbed
When it has lost touch with
  reality

When it is always about them
When it is unreasonable
When it is selfish
When it is not trustworthy
When it is controlling
When it is negative
When it always complains
When it is manipulating
When it wants it's own way
When it is disrespectful
When it is disgraceful
When it's no longer welcomed
When it's not appreciated
When it's not committed
When it's unholy
When it's self-righteous
When it's draining

H0W MUCH MORE OF IT CAN YOU TAKE?

You've tried to dress it up
  cover it up
Leave it
Ignore it
You've turned it upside down
  and inside out
When it still hangs around
When it mocks you
When it stalks you
When it's with you
  everywhere you go
When it hovers around you
When you're close to it
When you're related to it
When you love it
When it won't go away
When it is overdrawn
When it is overdue
When it is not enough
When it is depleted
When it is gone

When it doesn't sustain you
When you have outgrown it
When it's not good enough
When it lied
When it cheated
When it had an affair
When it went behind your
   back
When it was your friend
When it won't work
When it won't give
When it won't listen
When it's lazy
When it's a hustler
When it won't take
   responsibility
When it's at church
When it's in the pulpit
When it's in the choir stand
When you've drank it
When you smoked it
When you've shot it up
When you've snorted it
When it nearly killed you

STILL DEALING WITH IT?

When you can see it but
  can't touch it
When you can smell it but
  can't taste it
When it's your size but you
  can't put it on
When it's made for you but
  someone else has it
When it was your prayer
When it was your vision
When it was your dream
When it was your insight
You've lost sleep over it
It has cost you something

NOW THAT I THINK ABOUT IT

It is experience
You've wrestled with it
It gave you a limp
It almost took you out
You've paid dearly for it
It brought you to the end of
  yourself
It turned out to be valuable
It turned out to be
  irreplaceable
It is ancient
It is precious
Your tears are stored in
  heaven because of it
It is one of a kind
It is costly
It is priceless
It is my alabaster box
It is my life
It is experience working
  patience
It is strength
It is will power

It is being steadfast and
  unmovable
It is my ability to press
It is now my relationship
  with him
It is my praise
It is my worship
It is my gift
It is gratitude
It is my reasonable service
It is my joy
It is my peace
It is hope
It is comfort
It is my prayer
It is victory
It is deliverance
It's my message
It is a lifeline
It is all I have…It is all
I've ever needed
It is what I've carried
It is my gift
It is what I bring forth
It is my hidden treasure
It is what God births

through me
It is what he nurtured...all
along
It is what I find passion in
It is what I scream from the
mountain tops
It is the way
It is the truth
It is the light
It is the breaker
It is the anointing

NOW THAT I RECOGNIZE IT

I don't worry about it
I accept it
I can talk about it
I've found peace despite it
I am who I am because of it
I can see beyond it
I can testify about it
I can appreciate it
I was chosen for it and it
  was chosen for me

THE TRUTH ABOUT IT

You can make it
You can take it
Stand strong in it
Go on despite it
Be encouraged in it
Seek God through it
Find purpose in it
It happened for a reason
Allow it to make you better
There's passion in it
There's power in it
There's provision in it
It moves at your command
It is waiting on you to
  speak
It is waiting on you to come
  forth
It needs you to manifest
  glory in the earth
It wants to hear what you
  have to say
It has posed a challenge,
  are you up to it?
It needs your response

AND WHILE YOU WRESTLE WITH IT

It's in travail
It's moaning
It won't be comforted
It's out of control
It is a mess
It is off balance
It is weak
It suffers
It needs to be delivered
It longs for him
It longs for peace
It is not about you
Stop taking it personally
Stop worrying about it
Stop obsessing over it
See what it can be
Don't let it have the rest
  of your life

THE FATE OF IT

He died for it and he died
  for you
It was nailed to the cross
It can no longer claim you
  unless you let it
Cast it on him
And leave it
It was sentenced to death
Accept it
Believe it
And walk in it
It will lead you from
  religion to the kingdom
You thought it was over for
  you
You felt like there was no
  forgiveness for it
You felt that it would carry
  you to your grave
But it didn't

Get it right this time
    and let it go
Once and for all
    drop it
It may be your last chance
    once and for all…
Get over it!

It was hard...

*It wasn't easy. It's been
downright difficult at times...*

God has caused rain to fall upon my "IT"s All of the rough, hard, jagged places in my life…

Are wet now...the drought is over. It is over! A time of Revival...I know it by heart.